12-Bar Blues Solos

25 Authentic Leads Arranged for Guitar in Standard Notation and Tablature

by Dave Rubin

Check out these other great
Hal Leonard books by Dave Rubin:

Boogie Blues Riffs (HL00699621)

Easy Rock Rhythms (HL00699667)

12-Bar Blues Riffs (HL00699622)

Solo Blues Guitar (HL00699719)

Inside the Blues series:

Acoustic Country Blues Guitar (HL00695139)

Art of the Shuffle (HL00695005)

Birth of the Groove (HL00695036)

Blues Turnarounds (HL00695602)

Inside the Blues 1942 – 1982 Updated Edition (HL00695952)

Open Tunings for Blues Guitar (HL00695412)

Power Trio Blues (HL00695028)

Rockin' the Blues (HL00695491)

12-Bar Blues (HL00695187)

To access audio visit:
www.halleonard.com/mylibrary

Enter Code
1711-9668-8989-0230

Guitar: Doug Boduch

ISBN 978-1-4234-0742-3

7777 W. BLUEMOUND RD. P.O. BOX 13819 MILWAUKEE, WI 53213

In Australia Contact:
Hal Leonard Australia Pty. Ltd.
4 Lentara Court
Cheltenham, Victoria, 3192 Australia
Email: ausadmin@halleonard.com

Visit Hal Leonard Online at
www.halleonard.com

CONTENTS

A Brief History of the Guitar Solo

The first written solo in popular music appeared in W.C. Handy's "Memphis Blues," published in 1912. Called the "jass" (i.e., jazz), it acknowledged a distinctive characteristic that had been evolving in blues and jazz for roughly two decades, particularly in New Orleans. The improvised solo was what gave the music spontaneity, energy, and dynamics.

In the 1920s, Lonnie Johnson, the great blues and jazz musician whom B.B. King cites as the most influential guitarist of the 20th century, was playing sophisticated and funky acoustic single-note lines that became the benchmark for a generation of blues cats. When Robert Johnson (no relation) contributed to the popularity and acceptance of the 12-measure progression as the standard blues form in the late 1930s, the musical environment was ripe for the final element that would allow blues guitarists to compete on equal footing with horn players for solo space in ensemble situations: electricity.

In 1936, Gibson's groundbreaking ES-150 hollow-body guitar with matching amplifier made it possible for Charlie Christian, in jazz, and T-Bone Walker, in the blues, to forge the sound and approach for virtually every guitarist who followed. In the early 1940s, Walker conclusively established the blues tradition of playing an improvised guitar solo with expressive phrasing, building on Lonnie Johnson's pioneering efforts.

When B.B. King brought the art of the electric guitar solo into the postwar era with a remarkable fluidity based on supple string bending and vibrato, the nature of the blues changed almost overnight. Following his 1951 classic "Three O'Clock Blues," the harmonica and slide guitar, both holdovers from the prewar acoustic country blues era, began to assume second-class status as guitarists in Chicago and Texas rushed forward to emulate the "King of the Blues."

Originally intended to complement the vocal melody, blues solos have evolved to afford the guitarist the opportunity to make a personal musical statement, often with the added attraction of virtuosity in the hands of such players as Freddie King, Buddy Guy, and Stevie Ray Vaughan, to name a few. However, telling a "story" with your blues solo—with beginning, middle, and end sections—is still a worthy goal.

The 25 12-bar blues solos in this book attempt to demonstrate that concept in a variety of styles, including blues-rock, Latin, and funk, along with the expected slow-blues and shuffles. Learn them all and you will step into the spotlight at your next blues jam with authority and confidence. Enjoy and emote!

About the Audio

This book contains audio complete with demonstration and play-along recordings for each musical example. The Demo Track for each Solo includes both the written lead guitar and the accompanying rhythm guitar. The Play-Along Track contains only the rhythm guitar part so you can play along. To tune your guitar, use the tuning notes on Track 51.

Solo #1

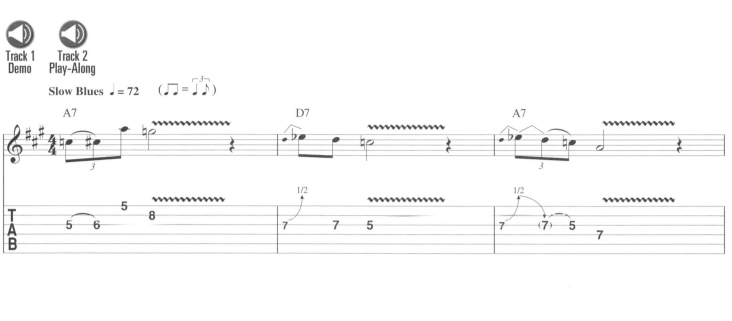

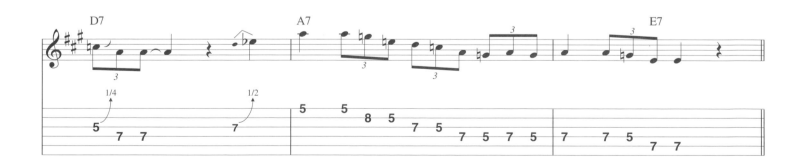

Solo #2

Track 3
Demo

Track 4
Play-Along

Slow Blues ♩ = 72 (♫ = ♩♪³)

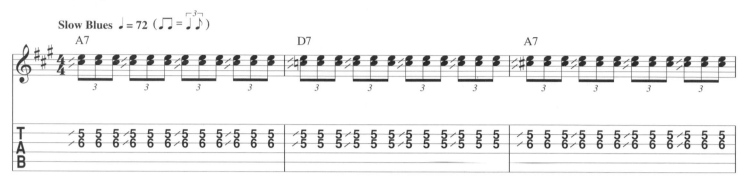

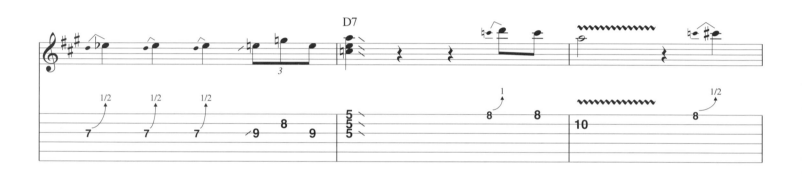

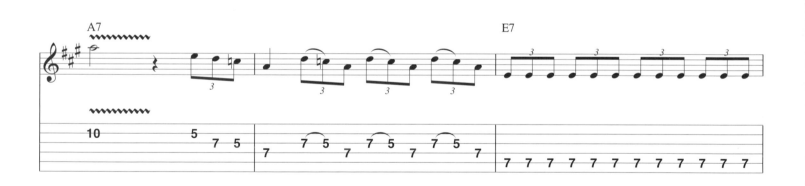

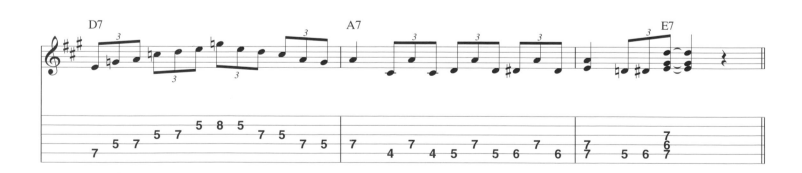

Solo #3

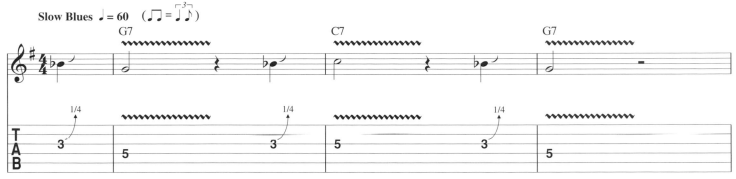

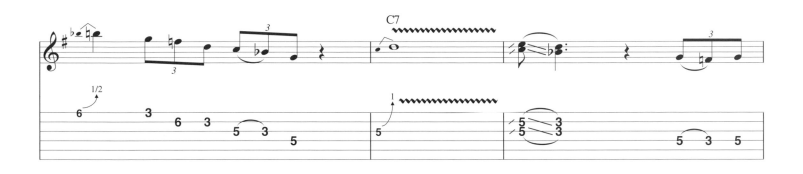

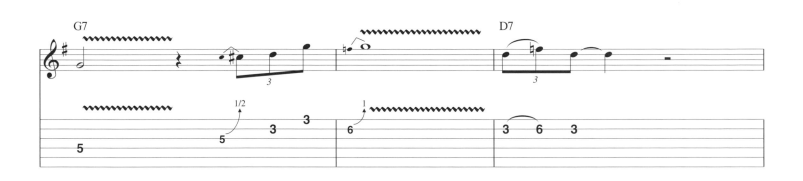

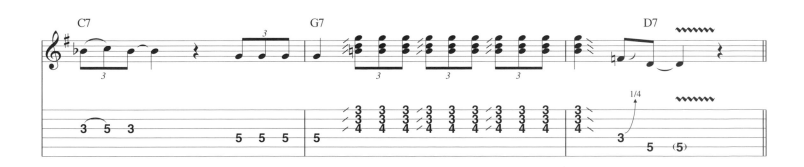

Solo #4

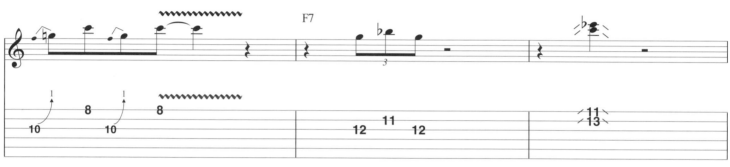

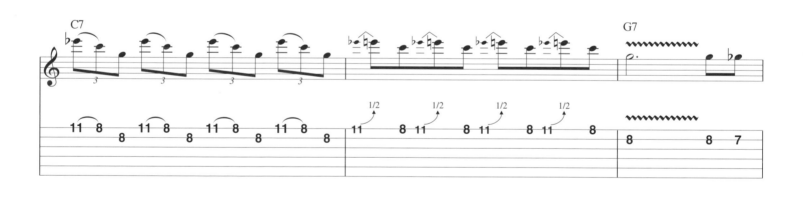

Solo #5

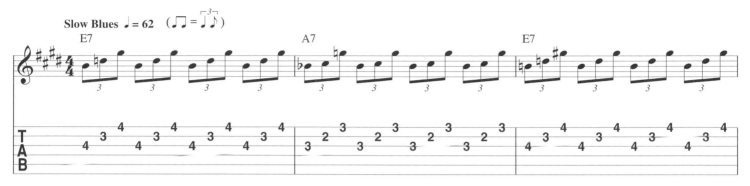

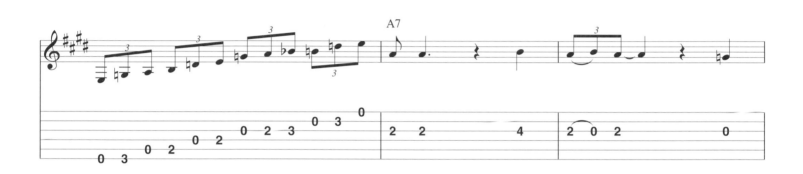

Solo #6

Track 11
Demo

Track 12
Play-Along

Moderate Shuffle ♩ = 84

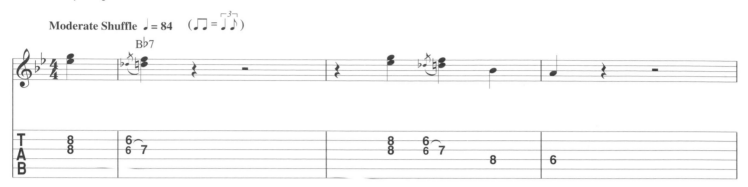

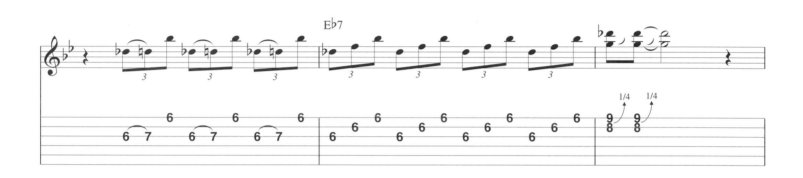

Solo #7

Moderate Shuffle ♩ = 100

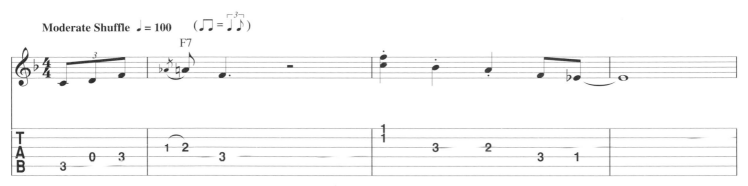

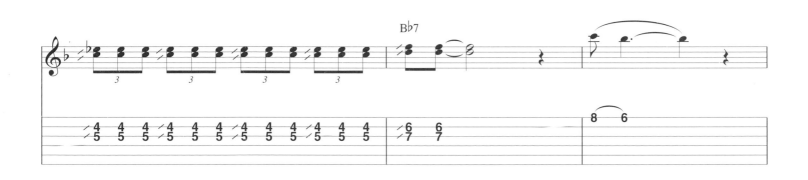

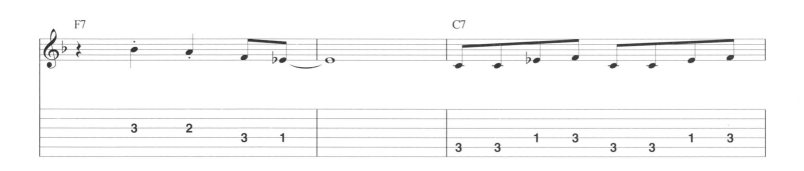

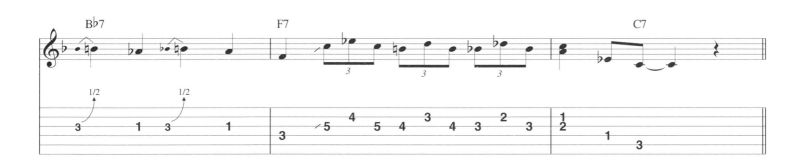

Solo #8

Track 15
Demo
Track 16
Play-Along

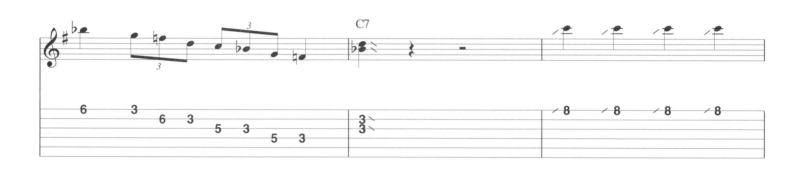

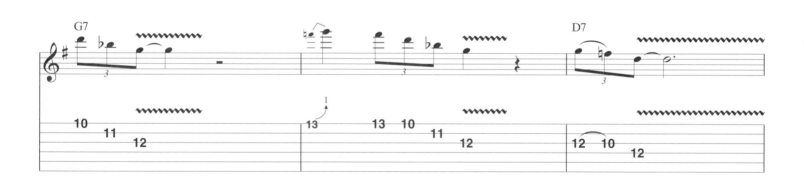

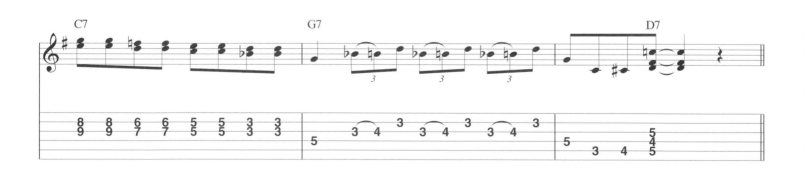

Solo #9

Track 17
Demo
Track 18
Play-Along

Moderate Shuffle ♩ = 100

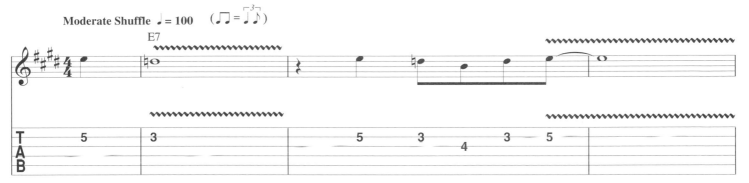

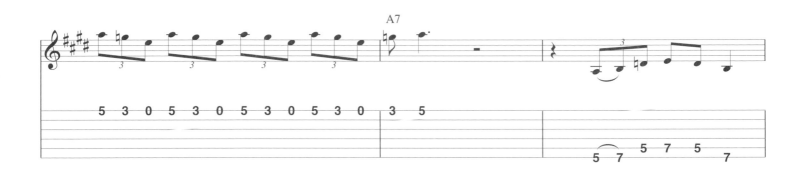

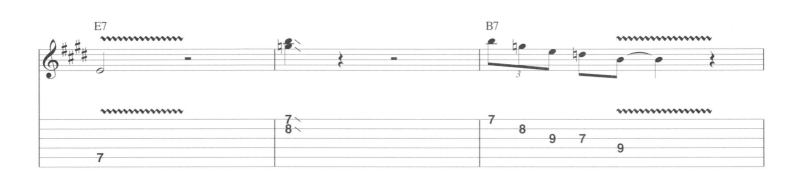

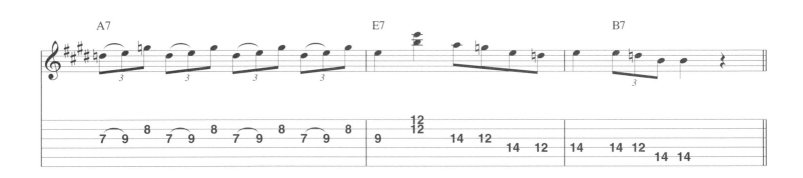

Solo #10

Track 19
Demo

Track 20
Play-Along

Moderate Shuffle ♩ = 104

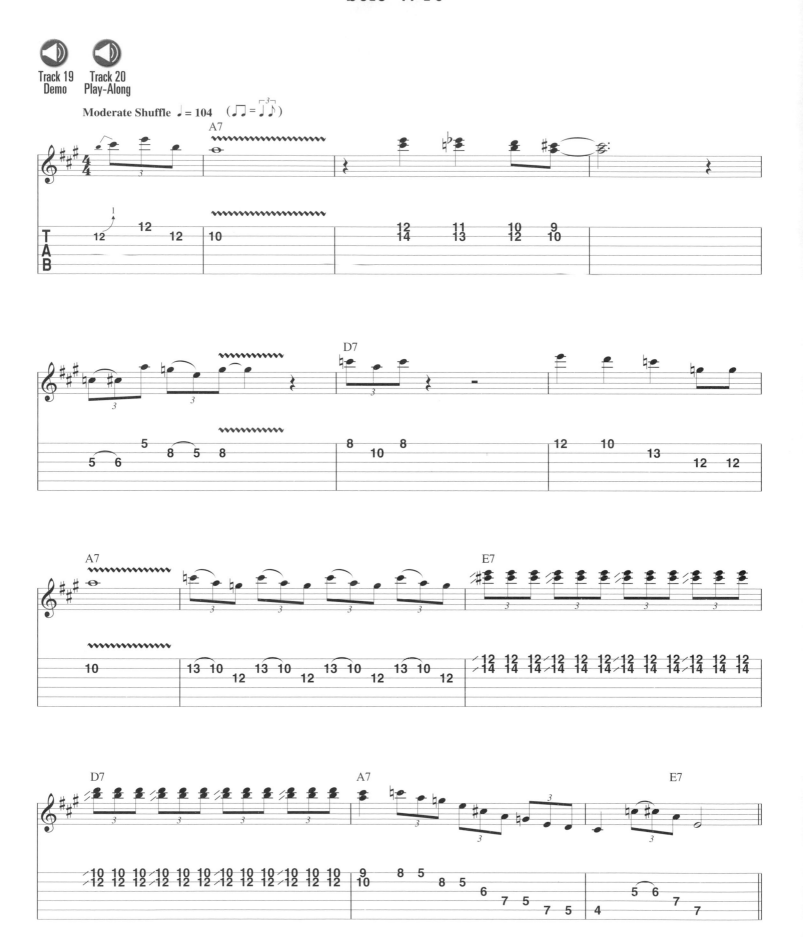

Solo #11

Track 21
Demo

Track 22
Play-Along

Moderate Funk-Blues ♩ = 100

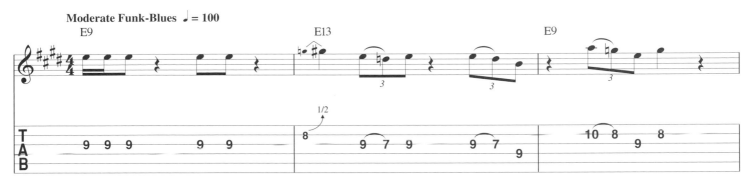

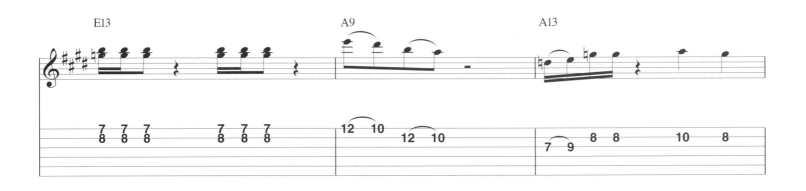

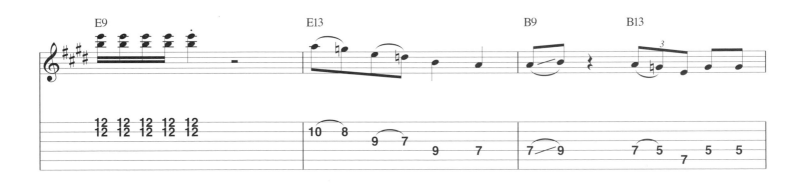

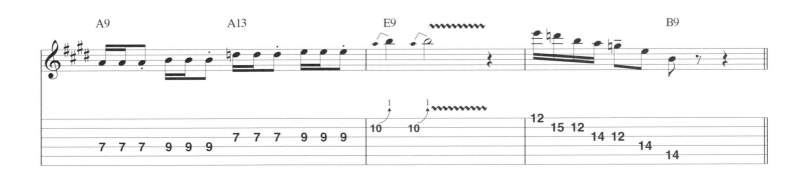

Solo #12

Track 23
Demo

Track 24
Play-Along

Moderate Funk-Blues ♩ = 102

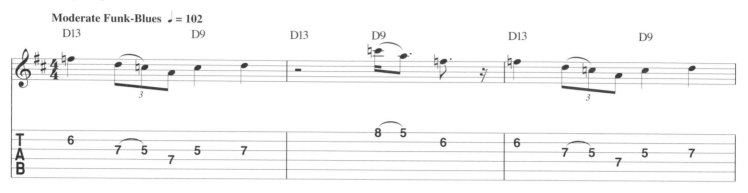

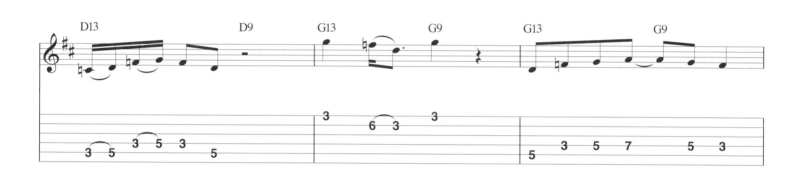

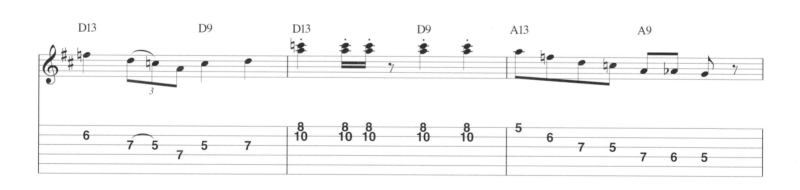

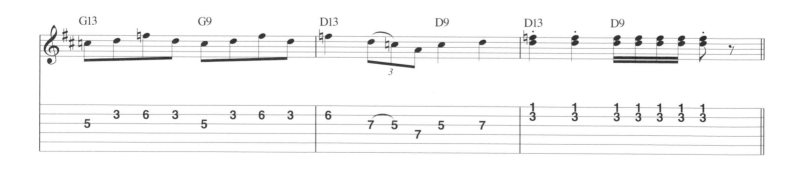

Solo #13

Track 25
Demo

Track 26
Play-Along

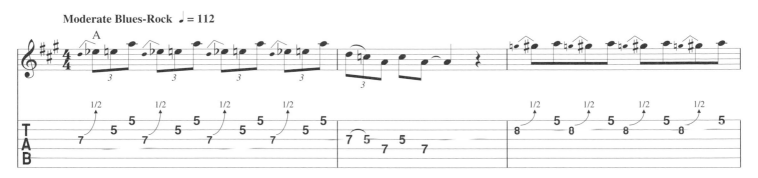

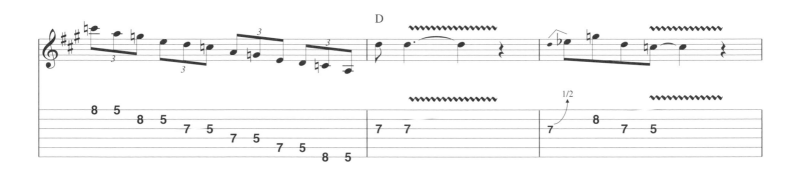

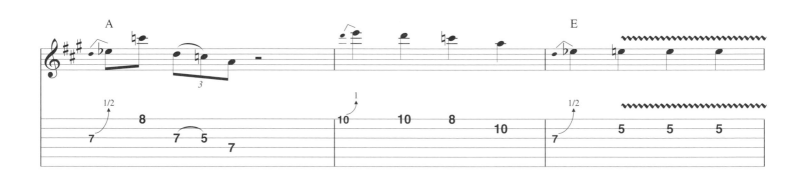

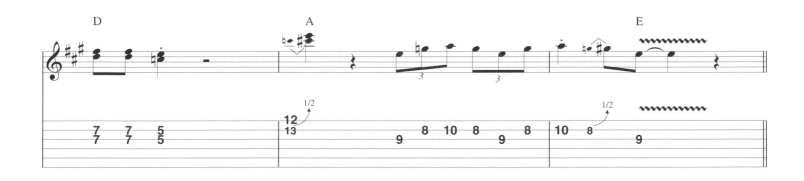

Solo #14

Track 27
Demo

Track 28
Play-Along

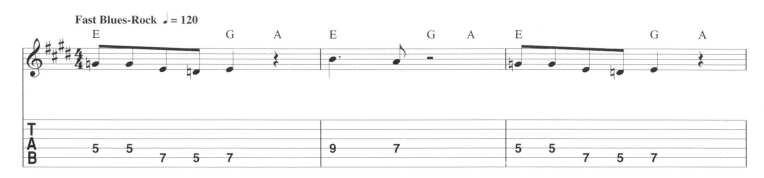

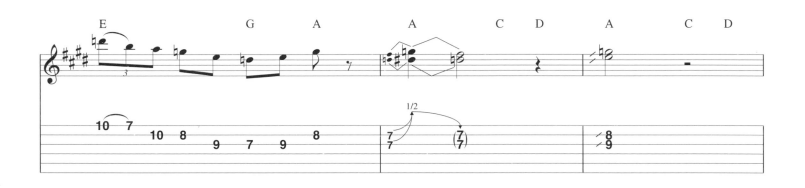

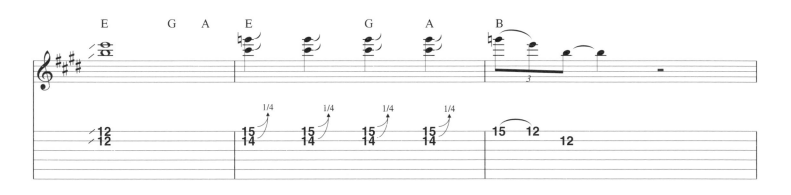

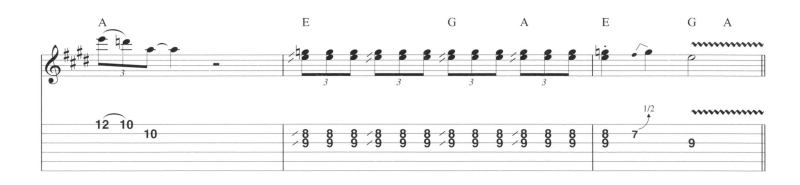

Solo #15

Solo #16

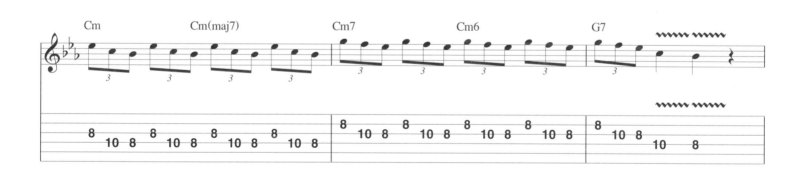

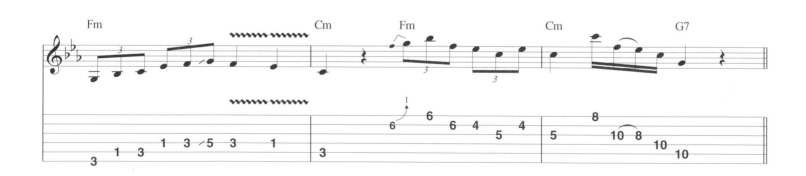

Solo #17

Track 33
Demo

Track 34
Play-Along

Moderate Latin-Blues ♩ = 108

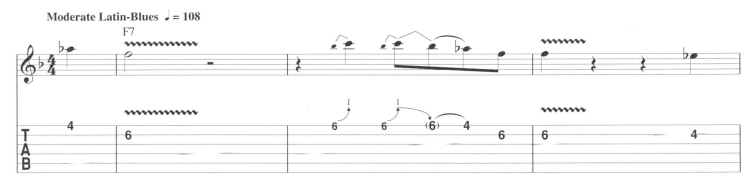

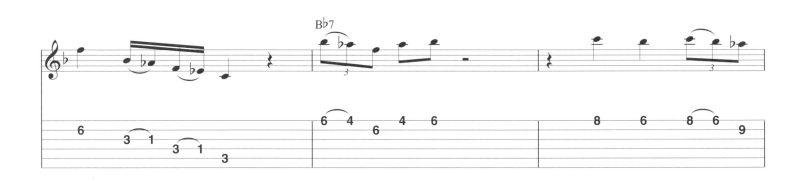

Solo #18

Track 35 Demo   Track 36 Play-Along

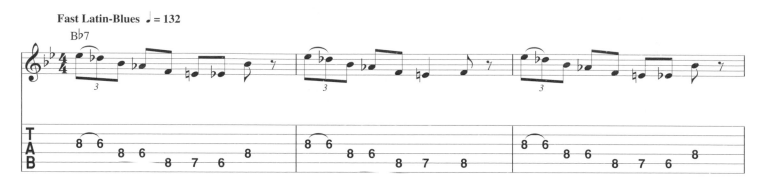

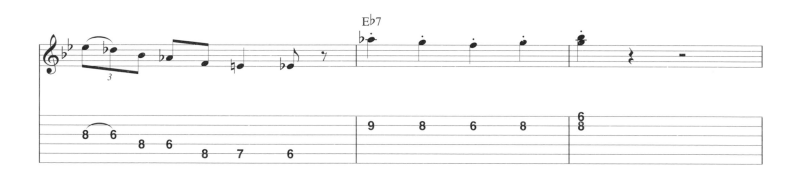

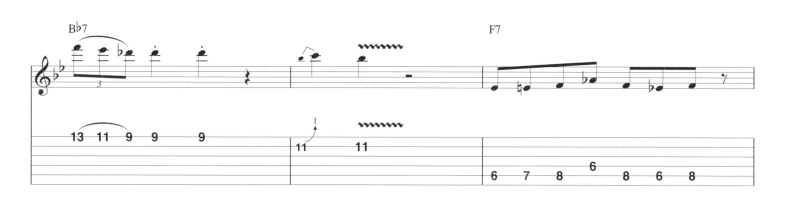

22

Solo #19

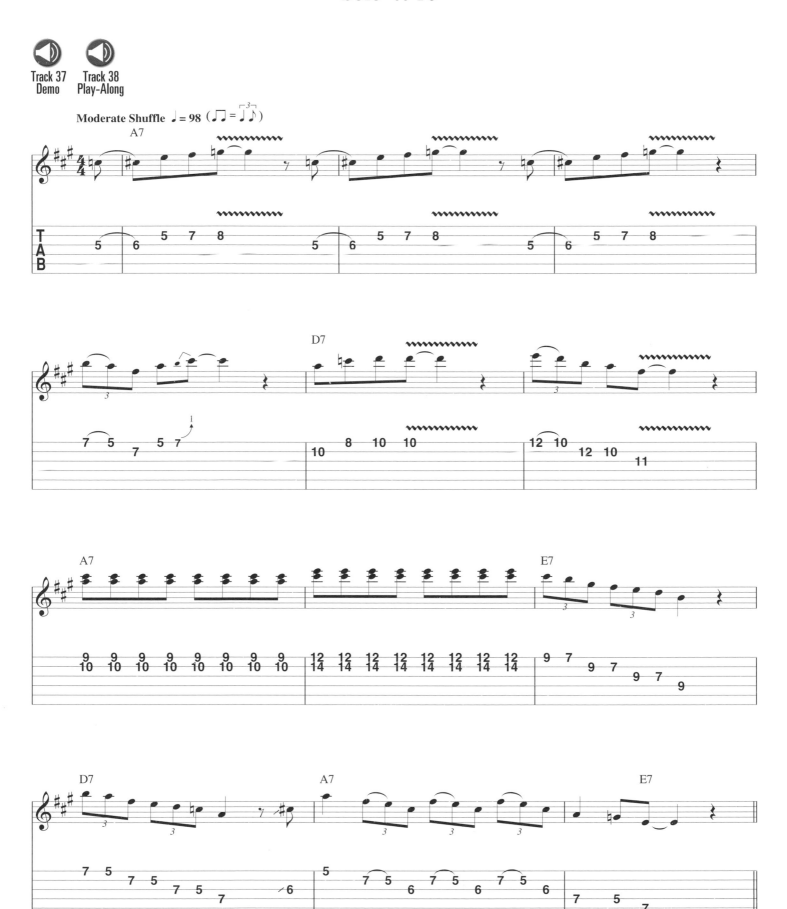

Solo #20

Track 39
Demo

Track 40
Play-Along

Moderate Shuffle ♩ = 112

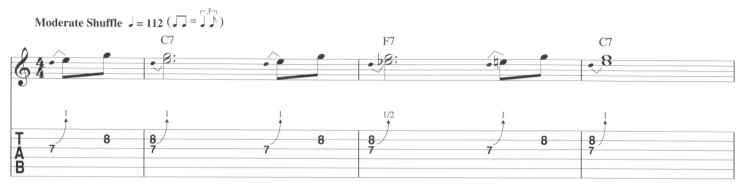

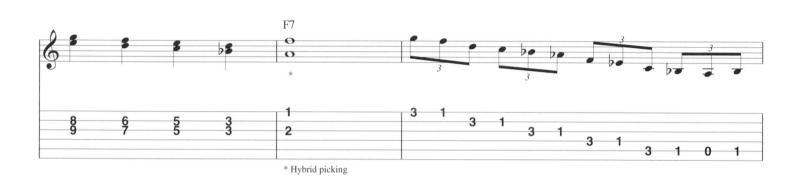

* Hybrid picking

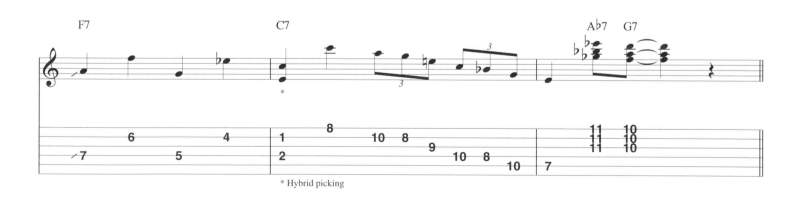

* Hybrid picking

Solo #21

Track 41
Demo

Track 42
Play-Along

Fast Shuffle ♩ = 122

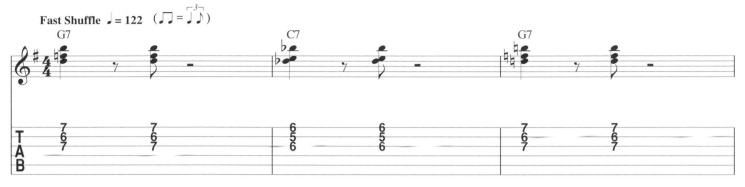

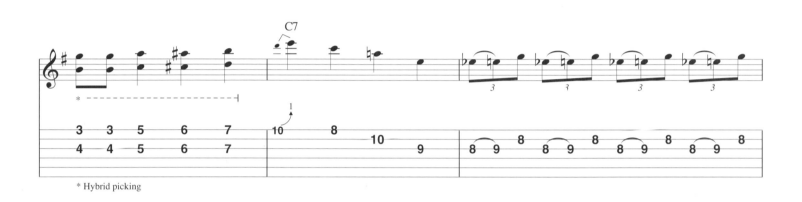

* Hybrid picking

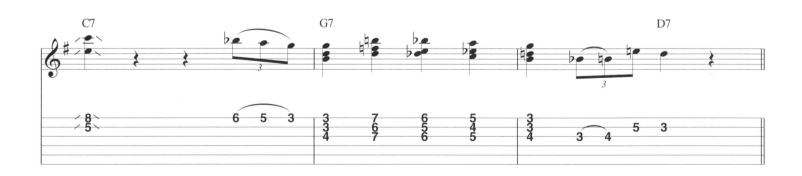

Solo #22

Track 43
Demo

Track 44
Play-Along

Moderate Shuffle ♩ = 108

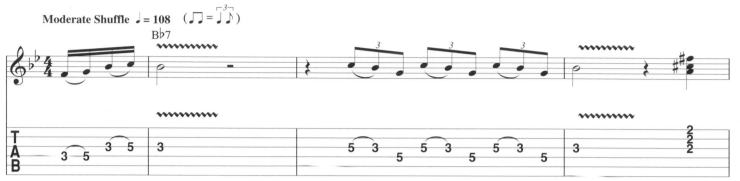

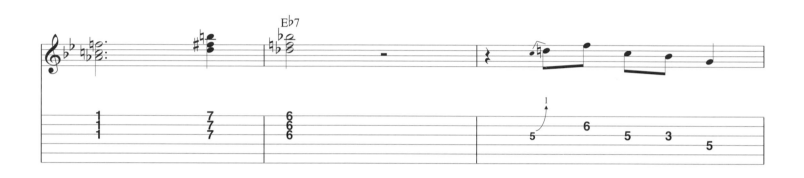

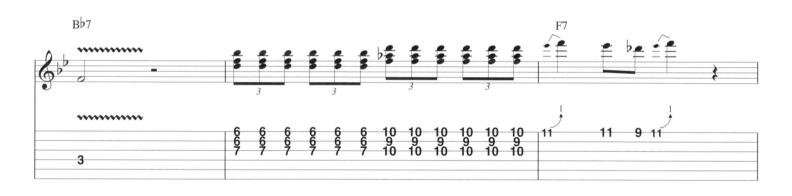

26

Solo #23

Moderate Shuffle ♩ = 120

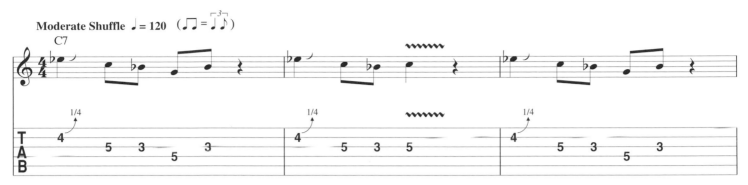

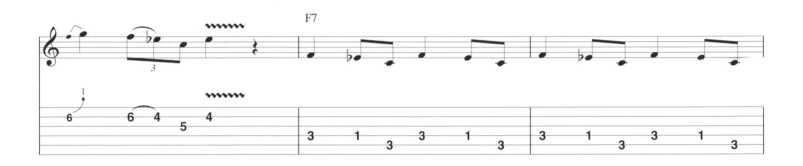

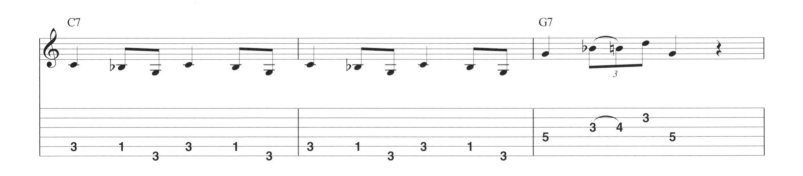

Solo #24

Track 47
Demo

Track 48
Play-Along

Moderate Blues-Rock ♩ = 112

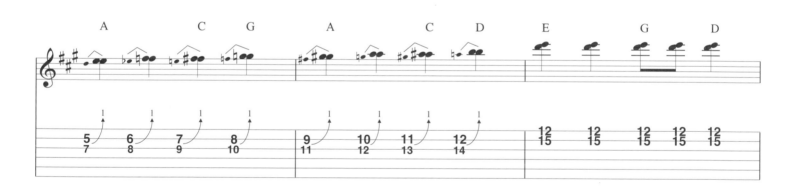

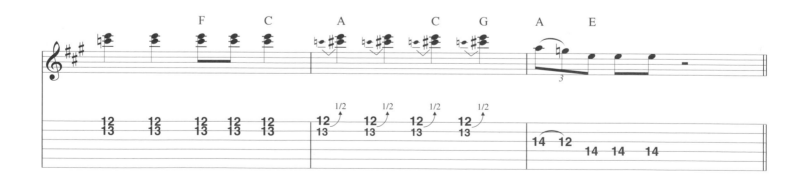

Solo #25

Track 49
Demo

Track 50
Play-Along

Moderate Blues-Rock ♩ = 124

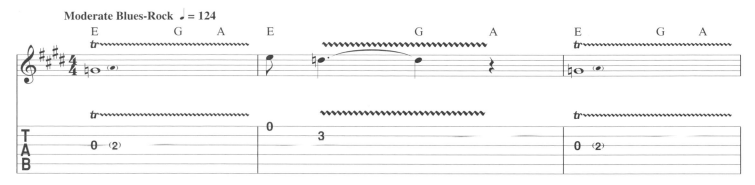

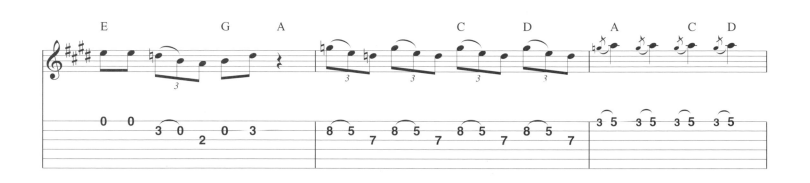

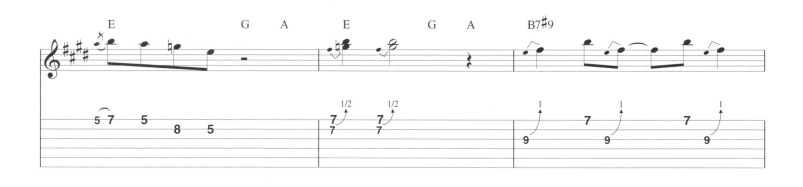

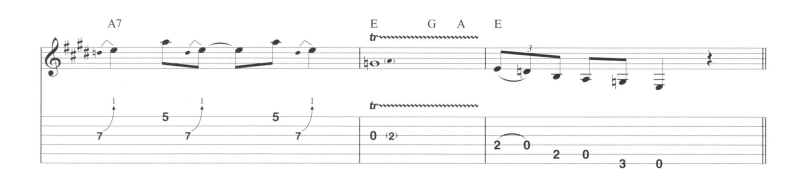

Guitar Notation Legend

Guitar Music can be notated three different ways: on a *musical staff*, in *tablature*, and in *rhythm slashes*.

RHYTHM SLASHES are written above the staff. Strum chords in the rhythm indicated. Use the chord diagrams found at the top of the first page of the transcription for the appropriate chord voicings. Round noteheads indicate single notes.

THE MUSICAL STAFF shows pitches and rhythms and is divided by bar lines into measures. Pitches are named after the first seven letters of the alphabet.

TABLATURE graphically represents the guitar fingerboard. Each horizontal line represents a string, and each number represents a fret.

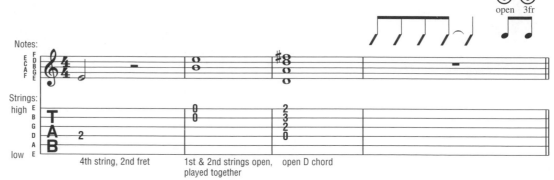

4th string, 2nd fret   1st & 2nd strings open, played together   open D chord

HALF-STEP BEND: Strike the note and bend up 1/2 step.

WHOLE-STEP BEND: Strike the note and bend up one step.

GRACE NOTE BEND: Strike the note and immediately bend up as indicated.

SLIGHT (MICROTONE) BEND: Strike the note and bend up 1/4 step.

BEND AND RELEASE: Strike the note and bend up as indicated, then release back to the original note. Only the first note is struck.

PRE-BEND: Bend the note as indicated, then strike it.

VIBRATO: The string is vibrated by rapidly bending and releasing the note with the fretting hand.

WIDE VIBRATO: The pitch is varied to a greater degree by vibrating with the fretting hand.

HAMMER-ON: Strike the first (lower) note with one finger, then sound the higher note (on the same string) with another finger by fretting it without picking.

PULL-OFF: Place both fingers on the notes to be sounded. Strike the first note and without picking, pull the finger off to sound the second (lower) note.

LEGATO SLIDE: Strike the first note and then slide the same fret-hand finger up or down to the second note. The second note is not struck.

SHIFT SLIDE: Same as legato slide, except the second note is struck.

TRILL: Very rapidly alternate between the notes indicated by continuously hammering on and pulling off.

TAPPING: Hammer ("tap") the fret indicated with the pick-hand index or middle finger and pull off to the note fretted by the fret hand.

NATURAL HARMONIC: Strike the note while the fret-hand lightly touches the string directly over the fret indicated.

PINCH HARMONIC: The note is fretted normally and a harmonic is produced by adding the edge of the thumb or the tip of the index finger of the pick hand to the normal pick attack.

PICK SCRAPE: The edge of the pick is rubbed down (or up) the string, producing a scratchy sound.

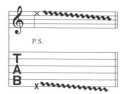

MUFFLED STRINGS: A percussive sound is produced by laying the fret hand across the string(s) without depressing, and striking them with the pick hand.

PALM MUTING: The note is partially muted by the pick hand lightly touching the string(s) just before the bridge.

RAKE: Drag the pick across the strings indicated with a single motion.

TREMOLO PICKING: The note is picked as rapidly and continuously as possible.

VIBRATO BAR DIVE AND RETURN: The pitch of the note or chord is dropped a specified number of steps (in rhythm) then returned to the original pitch.

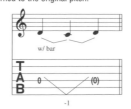

VIBRATO BAR SCOOP: Depress the bar just before striking the note, then quickly release the bar.

VIBRATO BAR DIP: Strike the note and then immediately drop a specified number of steps, then release back to the original pitch.

HAL·LEONARD GUITAR PLAY-ALONG

This series will help you play your favorite songs quickly and easily. Just follow the tab and listen to the audio to the hear how the guitar should sound, and then play along using the separate backing tracks. Audio files also include software to slow down the tempo without changing pitch. The melody and lyrics are included in the book so that you can sing or simply follow along.

INCLUDES TAB

Complete song lists available online.

Prices, contents, and availability subject to change without notice.

www.halleonard.com

0822
173

Get Better at Guitar

...with these Great Guitar Instruction Books from Hal Leonard!

101 GUITAR TIPS
INCLUDES TAB
STUFF ALL THE PROS
KNOW AND USE
by Adam St. James
This book contains invaluable guidance on everything from scales and music theory to truss rod adjustments, proper recording studio set-ups, and much more.
00695737 Book/Online Audio $17.99

AMAZING PHRASING
INCLUDES TAB
by Tom Kolb
This book/audio pack explores all the main components necessary for crafting well-balanced rhythmic and melodic phrases. It also explains how these phrases are put together to form cohesive solos. The companion audio contains 89 demo tracks, most with full-band backing.
00695583 Book/Online Audio $22.99

ARPEGGIOS FOR THE MODERN GUITARIST
INCLUDES TAB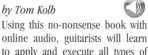
by Tom Kolb
Using this no-nonsense book with online audio, guitarists will learn to apply and execute all types of arpeggio forms using a variety of techniques, including alternate picking, sweep picking, tapping, string skipping, and legato.
00695862 Book/Online Audio $22.99

BLUES YOU CAN USE
by John Ganapes
This comprehensive source for learning blues guitar is designed to develop both your lead and rhythm playing. Includes: 21 complete solos • blues chords, progressions and riffs • turnarounds • movable scales and soloing techniques • string bending • utilizing the entire fingerboard • and more.
00142420 Book/Online Media................................$22.99

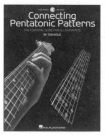

CONNECTING PENTATONIC PATTERNS
INCLUDES TAB
by Tom Kolb
If you've been finding yourself trapped in the pentatonic box, this book is for you! This hands-on book with online audio offers examples for guitar players of all levels, from beginner to advanced. Study this book faithfully, and soon you'll be soloing all over the neck with the greatest of ease.
00696445 Book/Online Audio $24.99

FRETBOARD MASTERY
INCLUDES TAB
by Troy Stetina
Untangle the mysterious regions of the guitar fretboard and unlock your potential. This book familiarizes you with all the shapes you need to know by applying them in real musical examples, thereby reinforcing and reaffirming your newfound knowledge.
00695331 Book/Online Audio $22.99

GUITAR AEROBICS
INCLUDES TAB
by Troy Nelson
Here is a daily dose of guitar "vitamins" to keep your chops fine tuned! Musical styles include rock, blues, jazz, metal, country, and funk. Techniques taught include alternate picking, arpeggios, sweep picking, string skipping, legato, string bending, and rhythm guitar.
00695946 Book/Online Audio $24.99

GUITAR CLUES
INCLUDES TAB
OPERATION PENTATONIC
by Greg Koch
Whether you're new to improvising or have been doing it for a while, this book/audio pack will provide loads of delicious licks and tricks that you can use right away, from volume swells and chicken pickin' to intervallic and chordal ideas.
00695827 Book/Online Audio $24.99

PAT METHENY – GUITAR ETUDES
INCLUDES TAB
Over the years, in many master classes and workshops around the world, Pat has demonstrated the kind of daily workout he puts himself through. This book includes a collection of 14 guitar etudes he created to help you limber up, improve picking technique and build finger independence.
00696587..$17.99

PICTURE CHORD ENCYCLOPEDIA
This comprehensive guitar chord resource for all playing styles and levels features five voicings of 44 chord qualities for all twelve keys – 2,640 chords in all! For each, there is a clearly illustrated chord frame, as well as *an actual photo* of the chord being played!.
00695224..$22.99

RHYTHM GUITAR 365
INCLUDES TAB
by Troy Nelson
This book provides 365 exercises – one for every day of the year! – to keep your rhythm chops fine tuned. Topics covered include: chord theory; the fundamentals of rhythm; fingerpicking; strum patterns; diatonic and non-diatonic progressions; triads; major and minor keys; and more.
00103627 Book/Online Audio $27.99

SCALE CHORD RELATIONSHIPS
INCLUDES TAB
by Michael Mueller & Jeff Schroedl
This book/audio pack explains how to: recognize keys • analyze chord progressions • use the modes • play over nondiatonic harmony • use harmonic and melodic minor scales • use symmetrical scales • incorporate exotic scales • and much more!
00695563 Book/Online Audio $17.99

SPEED MECHANICS FOR LEAD GUITAR
INCLUDES TAB
by Troy Stetina
Take your playing to the stratosphere with this advanced lead book which will help you develop speed and precision in today's explosive playing styles. Learn the fastest ways to achieve speed and control, secrets to make your practice time really count, and how to open your ears and make your musical ideas more solid and tangible.
00699323 Book/Online Audio $22.99

TOTAL ROCK GUITAR
INCLUDES TAB
by Troy Stetina
This comprehensive source for learning rock guitar is designed to develop both lead and rhythm playing. It covers: getting a tone that rocks • open chords, power chords and barre chords • riffs, scales and licks • string bending, strumming, and harmonics • and more.
00695246 Book/Online Audio $22.99

Guitar World Presents
STEVE VAI'S GUITAR WORKOUT
INCLUDES TAB
In this book, Steve Vai reveals his path to virtuoso enlightenment with two challenging guitar workouts – one 10-hour and one 30-hour – which include scale and chord exercises, ear training, sight-reading, music theory, and much more.
00119643..$16.99